BRIGHT
BUSINESS
IDEAS

Brian Lovig

ISBN 0-9697150-1-3

Published and Distributed by

Bright Publishing Inc.   Bright Publishing Inc.
Box 24002, Lakefront P.O.   Room 261, Box 5000
Kelowna, British Columbia   Oroville, Washington
Canada V1Y 9P9   U.S.A. 98844

Published Simultaneously in
Canada and
the United States of America

Library of Congress Catalog card number: 94-94485
Canadian Cataloging in Publication Data: Lovig, Brian, 1950.
Bright Business Ideas II. Includes index. ISBN 0-9697150-1-3.
1. New business enterprises, I. Title. HD62.7.L69 1994   658.1'1   C94-900259-3

Printed in Canada

Business books in the Bright Business Ideas series
by Brian Lovig

BRIGHT BUSINESS IDEAS

BRIGHT BUSINESS IDEAS II

To my wife who prompted me to write my first book and to my readers who asked that I write a second.

Contents   Page No.

Money Changer...10
Telephone Sweepstakes 13
Real Estate Sign Service...14
Jar Opener 14
C.D. Glove...17
Safety Deposit Book..18
Money Bags 20
Boot Planter...23
Name Association 24
Tea Sponge...26
Babysitting Kit..26
Ball Belt 28
Tan Tattoo...30
Bicycle Park...30
Business Climate Forecaster 32
Pen Pick 34
Table Talk..35
Hot Rock...36
Family Survival Pack 38
Compass Idea 40
Steering Wheel Notes 40
Television Cover...43
Auto Pool Service...45
Bread Rock..47
Mileage Meter..48
Horse Condominiums..51
Advice Sales Agent 52
Flyer Group 53
Special Occasion Service..54
Boat Store 57
Window Display Idea...58
Auto Consultant..60
Purse Holder 63
Parking Stall Condos...63
Restaurant Theme Idea...64
Bicycle Polo...68
Errand Service...70
Door Answering Machine 73
Hanging Tree...73
Parking Meter Pay Idea...74
Bike Bracelet 75
New Neighbor Video 76

Contents Page No.

Business Card Extra..78
Air Chairs...81
Phone Care Line 82
Computer Store Directory..85
Taxi Cab Confection Sales 87
Stilts...88
Picture Perfect..91
Sack Hat..93
Storage Condos 95
Craft Agent 101
Cheermitts 102
Sign Case 107
Postage Machine...108
Timely Investment 111
Fashion Helmet 112
Traveling VCR 115
Idea Consulting Sales Agent 116
Service Service 117
Pine Cone Fire Idea 118
Beard Trim Tray 120
Mobile Book Sales...122
Movers Group...124
Designer Paper Clip 127
Honey Novelty Sales 127
Message Band 128
Know-It-All Service 129
Pavement Message..130
No Auto Spill...130
High Rise Floor Condo 132
Umbrella Plate..134
Chimney Sweep 134
Valet Grocery Cart Parking 135
Story Glove...137
Briefcase Billboard 138
Invoice and Service Control Agent 140
Traveling Sports Shower 143
Board Game 144
Auto Television Network..146
Tire Use 148
Barrel of Fun...148
Barter Book 149

About the Author

Brian Lovig, born and raised on the prairies, now lives in the Okanagan Valley, British Columbia, north of Washington State.

At an early age and with little formal education Brian began a career in the auctioneering business. He has never restricted himself from exploring any avenue of business or from trying any venture. Along the way he has enjoyed many successes and gained valuable and practical business experience from each situation.

From creating names for new food products, trademarking and selling them to multi-national corporations, to buying and selling large tracts of land, apartment complexes and high-rise buildings, Brian has done it all!

His uncanny ability to come up with new concepts for development and novel ideas for marketing, has brought many people seeking assistance or guidance in sales and creativity, to his door.

Realizing that he had more bright business ideas than he could ever practically do on his own, his wife came up with the best concept of all – to publish some of his ideas in a book!

Brian's response to the success of his first book was to develop a series of business books. Bright Business Ideas II is the second in the series.

Foreword

Bright Business Ideas II is my second collection of unique money-making ideas. For as long as I can remember I have created new concepts and have worked towards enhancing existing ones. I have always enjoyed meeting with others to discuss their ideas and to work on new ventures. Many jobs, spin-off industries, and lifestyles have developed from innovative concepts. Our free enterprise system was created by and has prospered from, bright business ideas.

Throughout history, ideas have been rejected by others for being too complicated, too simple, or just for being too silly. But those with a vision refused to give up and were determined to succeed. Many of the great fortunes were made by those with bright ideas. Concepts in this book can be both financially and emotionally rewarding. Use the ideas as shown or use your imagination to build on the original idea. A proper business plan and its implementation are important. Investigate all aspects of any bright business idea.

The future belongs to those who question the present, those who do not hesitate to challenge established ideas, and those who pursue bright ideas of their own.

Happy ventures!

Brian Lovig

Money Changer

In the past it was common for train conductors, bartenders, bus drivers and milkmen to wear a change dispenser on their belt. Coins were separated into denominations and were easily dispensed for making change.

Idea: Introduce the money changer to the consumer market as a retail item.

Market: This is primarily a fad or trend item and the initial introduction should be targeted to those under 25 years. A more sophisticated money changer could also be developed for the executive market.

Product: Contact people in the hotel industry, railway or transportation companies for leads to an existing manufacturer. Updated versions of the money changer can likely be developed inexpensively and quickly. Another alternative is to design a money holder and take it to plastic companies for manufacturing quotes. Plastic holders may be less expensive. Fashionable colors would increase demand for the product. In your advertising, market them as accessories.

Marketing: Contact wholesalers and distributors to sell to retailers. Department stores, clothing, gift and variety stores are ideal sales outlets. Promotions can include a

(Continued on page 12)

new and unique fashion statement as well as a sensible way to control one's money. Consumers can be encouraged to own several money changers of different colors to coordinate with other outfits.

Potential:

There is a lot of potential with this product. It's unique, useful and could become a fashion trend. Determine the suggested retail price from researching consumers and retailers. Unique products often are able to earn higher than normal profit margins for the marketing company.

Possible Names:

Money Changer
Money Holder
Body Purse

The doctor examined the man who had swallowed the silver dollar and commented that there was no change yet.

Most clubs, associations and charities sell raffle tickets for cars, trucks, bikes, trips or other prizes. Ticket sales however, depend on viable selling locations and the availability of volunteers. Rather than relying on volunteers to access ticket buyers at booths or going door-to-door, why not take raffle ticket sales into the living room through television advertising by using a 1-900 user-pay telephone service?

The raffle would be advertised on television and the service or community club would announce the time, purpose, and value of the draw. They would also flash a 1-900 telephone number which could be called and the cost of the ticket would be billed directly to the caller. The telephone company pays for the ticket and the ticket is mailed to the caller, who then pays the telephone bill. All from the comfort of home!

The service club now has access to many more ticket buyers and no longer has to rely on so many volunteers. Everyone wins!

An obstacle is something you see when you take your eyes off the goal.

Real Estate Sign Service

Tens of thousands of real estate sales people each day deal with "For Sale," "Sold," "Reduced," and "Open House" signs; they put them up and take them down. Many of these realtors would rather avoid this tedious task. More important, it's time spent that could be better used.

Set up a real estate sign service to do all of the sign work. Contact realtors and arrange to deal with their signs. Establish rates and set out the details of the service offered. A realtor, accountant or an attorney would be helpful in the preparation of the business plan and structure.

A sure sign of success!

Jar Opener

Jars are often hard to open. Here's a product to do the job.

Use rough coated rubber and design circular jar openers in a variety of diameters and colors. Sell these to companies which then can stamp the openers with their own messages or advertisements and use them for promotional give aways. One example of a promotional message is:

> "Peter's Pickle Company, our gift to you
> ...better to open our great tasting pickles!"

Viable markets include anyone who sells jams, jellies, pickles and preserves. Personalized jar openers would be great gifts for anyone who does their own canning.

C.D. Glove

Compact discs (C.D.s) are popular and production and sales are constantly increasing. The music or sound face of the C.D. can be damaged. How about a C.D. glove?

Fashion a covering for part of the thumb and index finger and join them together. An alternative is to use a full-hand glove or a cloth with sewn areas for the thumb and index finger. Mount the C.D. glove on a solid backing, detail the use and package in clear wrap. Sales points include:

- to protect the C.D. from scratching
- the C.D. glove serves as a dust cloth.
- clean C.D.s produce better quality sound.

Present to retailers for conventional sales. Also present as promotional items. The retailer would screen their names, logo and numbers on the gloves. Sponsorship or advertising on the gloves from suppliers or entertainment companies is also a possibility.

This idea has an incredible "money sound!"

Possible names:　　C.D. Glove
　　　　　　　　　Clean C.D. Sound

Safety Deposit Book

Read any good books lately? This idea is hard to read... for burglars! Take a hardcover book and cut out a large area in about eighty percent of the pages. Money, jewelry or other valuables can be stored in this area and the book can be placed on a bookshelf or on a table.

Contact publishing companies or libraries for overstocked or out-dated hardcover books. Auction sales are also good places to find them. Telephone books could also be used. Obtain books at the best possible price,cut out the pages and sell the book! The now "safe book" could be sold for about $15.00. A profit of approximately $10.00 could be realized. Millions of homes and offices could use such a book! Sales can be made by wholesaling to retailers, or by mail order. Direct sales can be made at craft fairs or flea markets.

This is an ideal business for students or homemakers who require after-hours work. In addition, there is a great potential for profit.

A "safe" way to make money!

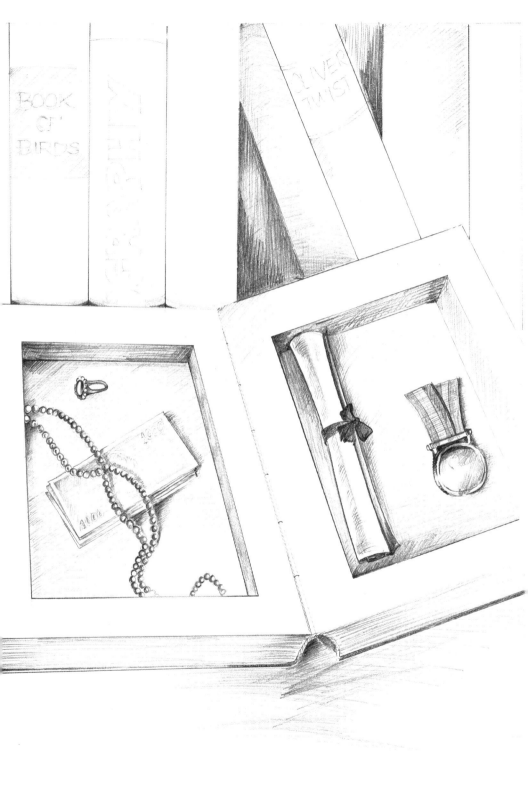

Money Bags

Change in purses or pockets can be heavy and inconvenient. It is much easier to pay for an item with paper money rather than counting out pennies, nickels, dimes and quarters. So often, people will put their change into several piles with one dollar in each, add them up so they know how much money there is and then pour all the change back into one pool. Here's an idea!

Size netting to hold various coins equalling one dollar and package them with elastic bands. Brightly colored netting would further encourage people to bundle up their change. Provide an illustration on the package which shows the convenience and fun of using such a product.

It would be quicker to hand several money bags to the clerk when buying a particular item and less embarrassing than counting change with a line of people behind you.

This product can be packaged for a minimal cost and could command a large profit margin. Present to convenience stores, gas bars and department stores for sale.

This idea is worth its weight in coins!

Possible Names: Money Bags
                 Loose Change Bag
                 Net Profit

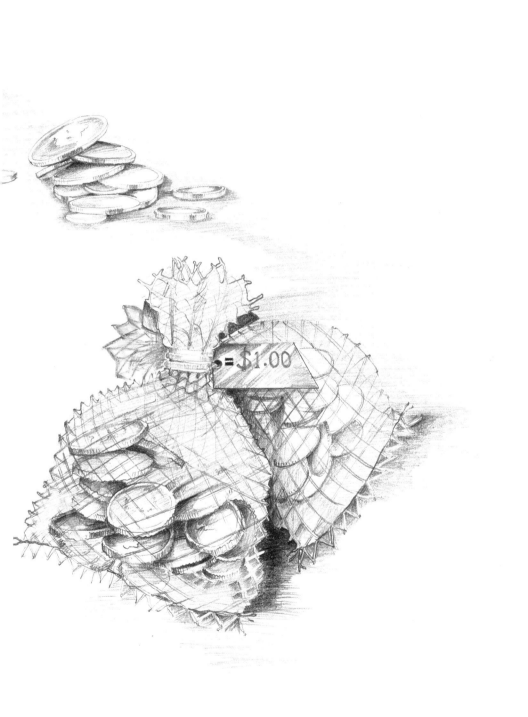

Collect old shoes, cowboy boots, work boots or running shoes and convert them into planters.

Treat them with a fibreglass resin mixture, available at hardware stores and lumber yards. Sell the boot planters with plants in them. Custom orders from clients with favorite footwear will be sure to be successful as well. Flowers or a plant in a marathon runner's shoe from a memorable race would be a great conversation piece.

Take brochures and samples door-to-door to solicit orders. Obtain the names of athletes from sports clubs and schools for a qualified sales list. A mall or roadside booth or flea market are also good places to sell. An organized sales program and product mix could be incredibly profitable!

You'll get a kick out of this one!

Possible Names: The Old Boot
Foot Loose
Boot Planter

You can't climb the ladder of success with cold feet.

Name Association

Search telephone books for surnames which match products that can be packaged to sell by direct mail, ie.: if the surname is Bird, prepare a brochure offering cards, ornaments and other products which make reference to their name. Items could include bird statues for the driveway, bird door knockers, etc. Think of the possibilities with surnames like Fox, Fisher, King, Knight and Star.

Results should be excellent because you target only qualified buyers. This mail order business can be operated from home and can be challenging and very profitable. Inventory does not have to be purchased until required to fill orders.

Possible Names: It's All in the Name
                   Surname Sales Service

You can't get to the top by sitting on your bottom.

Mr & Mrs Bird
11139 Cherry Lane
Minnesota

BIRD WALL CLOCK

BIRD COAT RACK
$11.95

BIRD MUGS. $9.95

573
The
BIRDS

BIRD
HALL

STATIONERY . $5.95
...TING PAPER . $12.95
...LOPES. $14.95

Tea Sponge

An all-wet idea! Even some of the best teapots drip or spill down the spout when being poured. Design a round sponge which can be slipped onto the spout to prevent this. Print a cardboard card describing the use and include an illustration. Shrinkwrap the sponge to the cardboard and another new product is ready for market!

Babysitting Kit

Prepare and market a kit for babysitters. This could be offered as part of a babysitting course or could be sold independently by retailers.

Design an attractive carrying tote with several compartments. Include a notepad for booking appointments and recording such information as children's names, parent's names and location, emergency contacts, household routines and special circumstances. An entertainment section could include storybooks, coloring books and crayons, puppets and perhaps a stuffed animal. A first-aid pamphlet and appropriate supplies is a vital component as well. Finally, include a ledger for recording money earned, dates, rates and client's telephone numbers.

The market is wide open for this one!

Ball Belt

What a ball!

Design a belt to hold tennis balls. The belt should be made of lycra and have an elasticized netted pouch attached to hold the balls. Select a variety of colors for the netting.

Market to sports stores, tennis clubs and recreation centers. Advertiser messages could be silkscreened on the belt. A ball belt eliminates the need for pockets and allows the player to carry more balls. A ball belt could hold up to six tennis balls comfortably.

Expand on this idea!

Change the size and materials of the ball belt to accommodate other uses.

Sports:
- golf balls and badminton birdies
- fishing gear

Homemakers:
- for household cleaners

Trades people:
- for tools

Waitresses:
- order book, pencil etc.

Teachers
    and students:
- chalk, markers, scissors, pencils, pens etc.

Hairdressers:
- scissors, combs, brushes etc.

Market to the appropriate retailer.

Tan Tattoo

Finally, a tattoo that can fade and disappear!

Design a variety of cut-outs that can be worn during a tanning session. The cut-out will block certain letters or pictures from tanning rays and when removed, will leave a lighter colored marking.

Present to distributors to sell to convenience stores, tanning salons and drug stores.

Bicycle Park

Here is an idea to complement today's emphasis on fitness. With increasing numbers of cyclists, the need for parking and security of bicycles has increased.

Design a compact bike rack, in components of four units, that is easily stored, transported and secured. See a locksmith and devise a coin-activated locking device like the ones used at bus depots for storing luggage. The user would insert coins and the key for the lock chain would be released. To retrieve the bicycle the key would release the locking mechanism.

Approach the city, malls, colleges, video stores and others for permission to put a bike rack by their building.

Cyclists now have parking facilities and you now have an exciting vending business!

Business Climate Forecaster

Hang a coin from a small stand with a base shaped to show printed instructions:

Coin Climate Forecaster:

If the coin can be seen, business will be good today (or it's daylight); if the coin is wet, watch out for slippery deals today (or it's raining); if you can't see the coin, today's business is unclear (or it's foggy); if it's moving, business will be brisk (or it's windy); and if the coin is gone, stay home, there's been a recession (or a tornado).

Package in clear plastic wrap and present to retailers. Sell at flea markets and auctions. The more elaborate the stand, the higher the price! Make it fun and profitable. Consider laminating a dollar bill and using it instead of a coin.

Always borrow from a pessimist. He doesn't think you're going to pay him back anyway.

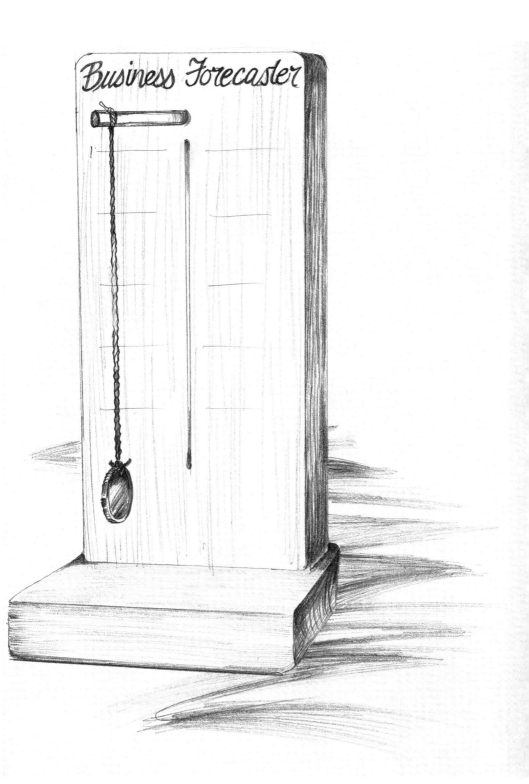

Pen Pick

Billions of toothpicks are used annually. These are sharp and often inconvenient to carry. Create a toothpick holder attachment for pens or a pen/pencil toothpick.

Attachment: Design a circular-type holder which can snap or clip onto a pen or pencil. One or two toothpicks can fit into the holder.

Pen/Pencil Pick: Push down and toothpick shows from stem. This is exactly like the pencils which are available now at retailers. The pen pick would produce a toothpick versus lead. It would also be returned inside the pencil when the top is depressed.

Contact pencil companies to see if they will custom manufacture pen picks. Negotiate prices and terms. This is also a great opportunity for them as they can sell their product into another market.

Marketing: Design displays suitable for restaurants and food stores. Also present these for promotional give-aways, ie.: a restaurant would provide a complimentary pen pick, complete with its name, slogan and address screened on the pen pick, to customers after their meal.

Possible Names: Pen Picks
Toothpick Pencil

Most homemakers have separate table settings for everyday use and for special occasions. This idea adds a third setting to a home's collection. How about an unmatched set of dishes for fun and conversation?

A setting for four could include plates from a world's fair, a rock concert, a city and a state! Cutlery could be in an assortment of sizes, with varying labels and from different places. Glasses and cups with various messages would complement these. Unique serving bowls and placemats could complete each set.

Another possibility is to design a tablecloth with food trivia. Include information about various foods too, ie.: Chinese and Italian. Describe the history of certain foods and other interesting points. Use humor and illustrations to further enhance the fun mood of the new table setting. Now there is much to discuss at meal time! This idea is great for entertaining new friends and neighbors.

These items can be obtained new from various suppliers or from flea markets and auctions. Package in boxes, label with information and illustrations and present to retail buyers.

Possible Names: Table Talk
                   Plate of Interest
                   Table Trivia

Hot Rock

Years ago rocks were heated in open fires and then were put into a pan of water to heat the contents. The idea is to package several small rocks with a bowl and tong set and to sell as a useable fashion item to homemakers.

Select round rocks and consider painting them in different colors with a non-toxic paint. Attach a printed card detailing the use and a brief history. Part way through a cup of coffee or tea, visitors would have the bowl of tiny hot rocks placed in front of them. When a rock is put into their cup, the contents immediately become hot again. What a conversation piece at coffee time!

Package attractively. Tongs, cups, placemats, and a bowl can be included with the rocks. Make up sample packages and present to retail buyers for their consideration. Other markets include craft shows and flea markets.

This idea could pick up steam!

Possible Names: Hot Rock
                    Coffee Rock

Family Survival Pack

Every home should be stocked with a survival kit in the event of a disaster.

Design a clearly labeled and compact container and fill it with appropriate food, first-aid, and emergency items. Market by direct mail and door-to-door sales. If properly priced and presented, people will respond very well to the product. Sell security and a form of life insurance versus doom and gloom. Who wouldn't pay a small amount for a survival pack for the sake of their family?

Other possibilities include developing custom survival packs for skiers and hikers.

Funny Money

The day after the last tax filing day is the day your income becomes a collector's item.

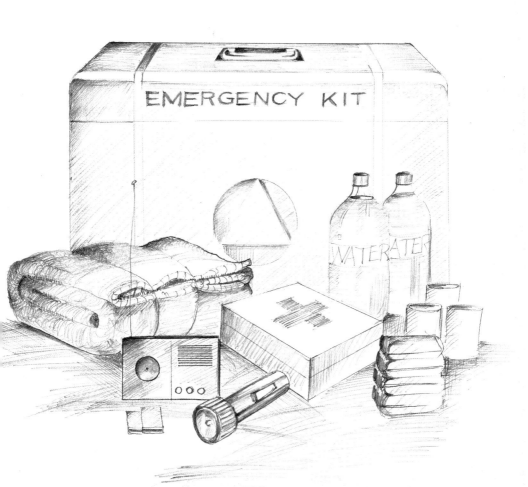

EMERGENCY KIT

WATER ATER

FLOOD
FIRE
EARTHQUAKE
SURVIVAL KIT

Compass Idea

Often, people are unsure of the direction they are going. Design a fashion item incorporating a compass. It could be on a watch, the watch strap, a ring or as an attachment to a shoe. While compasses are readily available, they are not common as regular wear.

Contact manufacturers and suppliers of compasses for prices and product types. Design a marketing program to create awareness of this "fashion product." Market the product showing runners, hikers, campers, shoppers and business people as users of the compass. Set up a display at gift and other trade shows to solicit orders.

Retailers should like an old/new item that is in fashion as well as having a practical use.

A "new direction" for making money!

Steering Wheel Notes

So often one needs to note something on a pad while driving. This idea lets drivers keep their eyes on the road.

Custom make magic slates to fit various steering wheel styles. Design them so that notes can be easily written while traveling. Now the driver can make notes and still drive safely!

Sell to office supply companies, gift shops and department stores.

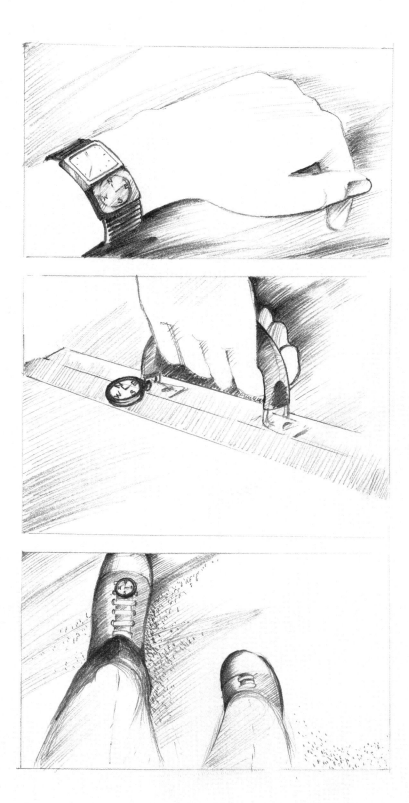

Often, students do their homework where the television set is. When it is on, this is quite a distraction! This idea keeps the television off and is an effective and fun way to control household habits.

Product:
A television cover. Design a plastic or paper cover that fits on the screen of a television set. This can be secured by the shape or static of the television screen. Design covers for a variety of screen sizes. Another option is to attach a cover to the cabinet to hang over the screen. Suction cups or weights would be effective. The cover could have a particular saying printed on it or be blank in the center where messages can be written, ie.: "Remove only after all homework is completed to the satisfaction of the household parent committee."

Advertising:
Consider selling advertising for the perimeter space of the cover. Potential advertisers include: Toy stores, video stores and pizza places.

Packaging:
Sell three or four covers in a roll or tube. Product and sales information can be printed on the outside.

(Continued on next page)

43

Market:

In addition to students, newlyweds and seniors can also be targeted as virtually everyone has a television. Many television messages can be created for these markets!

Marketing and
Distribution Plan:

• Sell via conventional outlets such as drug stores, department stores, television shops and at video stores.
• Organize and mobilize a direct sales team for door-to-door sales. Students or service clubs would be very effective.

Possible Names:

Life Cover
TV Control
Quality Time Cover

This idea is to establish a service for travelers that offers a benefit to those with or without a vehicle.

The auto pool service would take information and make this available for a potential match to others, ie.: A person without a vehicle who wishes to travel to another city would inform the service of the day of travel and of the amount of money that can be paid. Prior to driving to this same city, a motorist calls the service, learns of the other, and chooses to be accompanied on the trip. If the amount paid was one-half of the bus fare, the passenger realizes a fair savings, the motorist is rewarded and the auto pool service makes a profit.

The service would be responsible for screening its applicants, ie.: consider criminal and reference checks.

Charge a fixed amount from each party as well as an annual membership fee. A billboard illustration of a well-dressed customer will place the image of the service at the executive level. The potential for this service is great because people often restrict their travel due to costs. On membership cards, give a toll free telephone number to be used to organize travel. A computer, telephone operators and membership sales are all you need!

Possible Names: Safe Trip
                   Auto Pool Service
                   Automobile Travel Agent

Remember those pet rocks and how many of them sold? How about a bread rock? Here's how to use this idea.

A rock about the size of a dinner roll can be heated in the oven shortly before heating bread and rolls. When removed from the oven with tongs and placed in a bread basket it will keep bread and rolls warm.

Consider painting "Bread Rock" and instructions on the rocks so they can be sold without packaging. An option is to wrap the bread rocks and tongs in colorful and interesting baskets. Include an illustration and instructions for use.

Approach retail outlets such as gift stores and kitchen specialty shops.

Possible Names: Rock and Rolls
                    Bread Rock

Those who hide their heads in the sand won't leave any footprints on it.

Mileage Meter

Have you ever wondered how far you walked in a day? During a shopping trip? This is a practical fashion idea.

Put a mileage meter on shoes or a wristband. Contact automobile or computer manufacturers for advice regarding an appropriate product. Sell to shoe and department stores. Present to running shoe manufacturers who can attach the meter to their shoes. Advertise on the meters, ie.: "1000 miles or your money back."

This is a fun idea that can make a lot of money!

Possible Names: So Far, So Good
                   High Miler

The once successful businessman complained that his was a painful operation... he had his credit cut off.

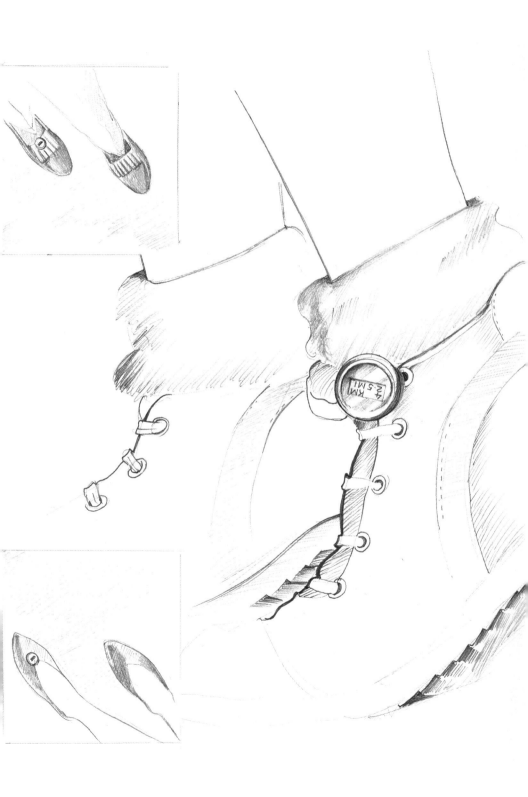

LUNGING RING

STRATA
UNIT
INCLUDES:
· STALL
· TACK ROOM
· PADDOCK

·STALL
·CHANGE & TACK
ROOM

COMMON

INDIVIDUAL
PADDOCKS

PARKING

BBQ

GATE

MANAGERS
RESIDENCE

Horse Condominiums

Many of us would love to own a ranch so we could keep a horse. This is difficult because of the hundreds of thousands of dollars needed to buy the property. The maintenance and management costs for the facility are also a major consideration. Few people can afford or justify buying a ranch.

How about a horse condo? This could provide virtually everything a private ranch could, without the cost! Each condo would have its own corral, a common pasture, barn and a tack room. A horse condo could be sold for up to $30,000.00, depending on location and land size. Condo fees could pay for maintenance and horse care.

Search for a parcel of land that's close to a park, field or similar area which is available for riding. As little as one acre would be suitable for the development depending on the location and size of other properties that can be used by the condo owners. Secure the selected property and prepare a site plan showing the layout of the buildings and corrals. Do the construction cost estimates and the sales projections.

Begin selling, using a model for the project or drawings. A real estate firm can assist with pricing, advertising and sales.

Don't horse around with this bright idea!

Advice Sales Agent

Speak your mind for profit! Produce and sell videos with advice or expertise from specialists in a particular area of interest. Some examples are:

Running:
Advise on what type of shoes are best, when to discard them, diets, clothing types and styles, training programs, running club names and locations, running publications, race locations and times.

Horses:
Advise on types and prices of horses, their costs, and how to care for them. Discuss the difference in styles and equipment for English versus Western riding. A feature topic like trail riding or polo playing would add fun to the topic!

Telephone Companies:
Advise on phone company's services; how to lower costs, the best times of the day to phone etc.

Computers:
Advise on what to buy, where to buy it and what to expect to pay. Discuss best system for various uses.

Advice can be sold for many more topics. Approach specialists in business, health, religion, education, automobile, sports and recreation groups with the idea of producing a video. Charge a fee for production and also a minimum of 10% of video sales.

Each video could feature up to three topics. Sell or rent these via mail order. A marketing feature is that video viewers can receive advice from the comfort of home.

There's no business like show business!

Flyer Group

An advertising flyer that is inserted in newspapers is an effective advertising method. This is costly and therefore limited to certain businesses. Set up a company to co-op advertising with a variety of companies into one flyer. Organize insertions with selected newspapers. Charge an agency fee from the client and a commission rate from the newspaper company. Your clients can now benefit from this type of advertising.

Special Occasion Service

Establish a business that contacts employees of companies on special occasions, ie.: the arrival of a new baby, birthdays, anniversaries and holidays. Letters of sympathy should also be sent.

Present a plan to businesses that would show the many reasons for them to establish a budget for your services. Incorporate into your fee the cost of postage, cards, and gifts.

When employees and their families receive cards and gifts for special occasions, morale will soar! This service contributes to strengthening the relationship between the company, the employee and their families.

This is a great idea for all companies regardless of their size. When properly presented, businesses will be glad that this service is available to them because it offers a fresh and personal approach to their business and ultimately benefits them.

Prepare a plan, research the number of businesses and employers in your anticipated market and then have a lot of fun and make a lot of money.

Possible Names: Calendar Control Service
                   Special Occasion Service

So you need to work but you want to enjoy the summer sun? Stock a small motor boat with newspapers, paperback books, watermelons, suntan lotion, sunglasses, cold drinks, gum and candies.

Boat up and down the shoreline of local lakes to sell to homeowners, boaters, campers, public-beach users and marinas. Advertise with a ringing bell and a printed sign on the boat. Signs at boat launch areas and rental docks would advertise your services and general location of the boat store throughout the day. Create an advertising board on the boat and sell advertising. Potential clients include beverage companies, marinas, and advertisers of local events.

Basically a floating confection store, this idea is unique and easy to expand.

Hire students and "flood" the market!

Possible Names: The Sale Boat
                   Convection Water Sales

Window Display Idea

An appealing and interesting window display for any retailer is an absolute necessity! Business people do not always have the props, time or ability to create effective window displays. Nevertheless, they are vital to advertise goods and constantly require fresh and innovative ideas.

Establish a window display company, specializing exclusively in window displays. Be creative and custom design displays for all types of businesses. Prepare brochures that include seasonal displays so that clients can pre-order. Potential clients include banks, investment companies, gas stations, clothing stores, supermarkets and art galleries.

Cooperative "window exchanges" would also be effective, ie.: display goods from a drug store in the window of a clothing store and vice versa. An exchange pool would provide extra advertising. Signs would indicate the location of the other store and other points of interest. Contract each client for long time periods to ensure a strong financial base.

Prepare a business plan, establish rates, prepare brochures, and contracts, and then present your service to retailers. This idea is exciting and can make money.

Possible Names: Picture Perfect Display
                    Window Display Creations

Auto Consultant

Advertise in classified auto ads and magazines that your company will do inspections to help select quality and dependable used vehicles for potential buyers.

Seek mechanics and others with expertise in the auto industry who will work as consultants on a per-job basis. Match auto consultants with auto buyers. Charge clients a flat fee or hourly rate depending on the type of inspection required.

Millions of used cars are purchased each year and buyers will welcome your services. Happy Motoring!

Possible Names: Auto Check
                    Auto Safety Test

Nothing is dirt cheap anymore, except gossip.

Purse Holder

A lady's purse is often set on the floor when she is in a restaurant or attending social events. This is inconvenient and the purse is literally underfoot. The bottom of the purse gets dirty and then is placed on her lap to be opened. This can stain clothing.

Design a holder that can be conveniently attached to the edge of a table so that a purse can hang from it. The holder can be the size of a large coin with a folding hanger as part of it. This can be easily carried in the purse.

See an engineer and a plastic company for design options. Present a prototype to department stores and ladies' fashion shops.

Parking Stall Condos

In most cities monthly parking is scarce and renting stalls is costly. Here's an idea.

Acquire or develop a parking lot and sell the individual spaces. Sales features include the guarantee of a parking stall, cost control and investment potential. Purchasers can also make money by renting their space to others and by re-selling it.

Locate the property, do the financial projections, speak to a surveyor and an attorney as well as approach the city with your plan. Although best suited for large cities, this concept will work in small centers as well.

This is a concrete idea!

Restaurant Theme Idea

Simply the best!

Theme:　　　　　To provide high quality meals by pro-moting certain food growers, manufac-turers and suppliers. Endorse particular companies and acknowledge that their meat, condiments and vegetable pro-ducts are "The Best!" Food companies have worked for a long time to establish their product, its quality, and reputation. Use their success to create your own. Serve the best food from the best place via the best company with the best ser-vice and price by the best restaurant!

Design:　　　　　The interior design should include illus-trations, photos and news clippings of the products and companies involved. A history of the origins of the products and companies would also be fun and inter-esting. Details of the founders, employ-ees and the service companies used would also be interesting. Photos and displays will add to the information and entertainment for the customer. Have a large "The Best!" sign by the information of each product or company. Consider an award certificate like, "We serve only the best and we have determined and selected this product as THE BEST. Annual reports and other available in-

(Continued on page 66)

The BEST FAMILY RESTAURANT

SERVING ONLY THE BEST NAME BRAND PRODUCTS

formation for any of the companies could be set out for reading.

Menu:

Design a menu with illustrations to accompany each food item. Illustrate and give details of the condiments. At the end of the menu, thank the customer and say something like, "Customer, you're the best!"

Marketing:

Contact suppliers for advertising money to assist in promotion. They should be receptive. Only suppliers whose products are accepted are stated to be the best. Publicity will also be available. It's news when only all of the "best" products are together for dinner.

Funding:

Select a location. Prepare a business plan complete with drawings and present to potential suppliers. Ask for prepayment of advertising money and indicate that the funds will be used for start-up costs. The nature of this concept makes the possibility of funding unique. As well, approach conventional lenders.

Potential:

This restaurant theme has great potential as a unique business. Additional locations possibly could be totally financed by suppliers anxious to be endorsed as "The Best!"

Possible Names: Simply The Best Restaurant
Best Brand Cafe
Best Restaurants

Bicycle Polo

Who needs a horse? Organize bicycle polo team games and a league. The rules should be similar to horse polo. Select a flat, grassy field and mark two eight foot goals at each end. Have three or four players to each team. Use shorter polo mallets and a soft ball about five or six inches in diameter.

Once several teams are assembled, devise a game schedule and release it to the press. Advertise the sport, charge admission and sell advertising using billboards at the playing field. Approach helmet manufacturers, bicycle shops and sporting goods stores for team sponsorships. Provide a concession stand at the games. Consider charging a fee to players for additional profit. Triathlon clubs and cycle shops are good places to find polo players for teams.

This could be an exciting new sport and it fits today's outdoor athletic lifestyle!

Funny Money

Most people would be happy to pay as they go if they could only catch up on paying for where they have already gone.

Errand Service

Business people have many daily errands. This may include going to the bank for cash or to make a deposit, picking up drycleaning, attending traffic court or a tax appeal, getting the mail etc. A competent errand service would free business people to spend their time more effectively.

Establish an errand service. This will occasionally parallel the services of a courier service as some of the work will be delivering or picking up items. The concept here, however, is to do errands and deal with certain affairs on behalf of the business or individual for whom you work.

This is a great business to start on your own. To get started advertise in the newspaper and with flyers. Contact small businesses personally.

Schedule yourself with clients throughout the day. Be on time for each appointment, do the job and go on to the next. Charge an hourly rate or consider having a contract with clients, thereby receiving a financial retainer to ensure use. This business can be run from the home with virtually no overhead.

The postal service will never issue a stamp honoring the inventor of the fax machine.

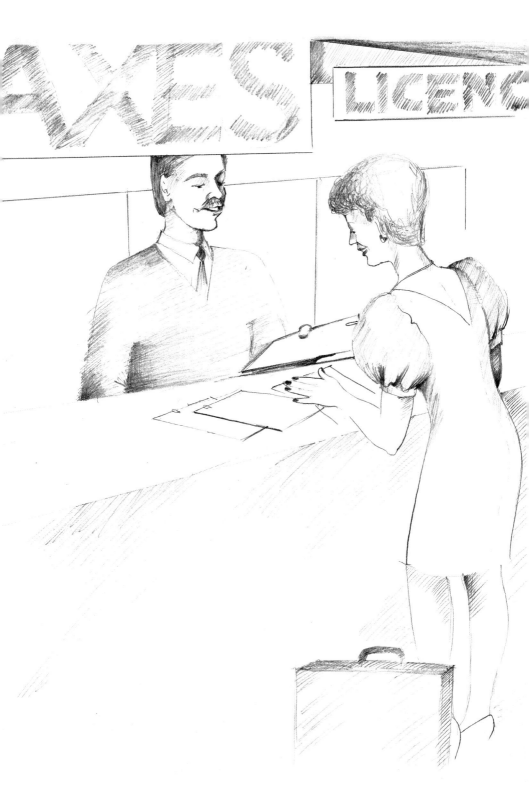

Door Answering Machine

It's common to be able to leave a telephone message on a machine, so why not at a door?

Approach electronic companies for styles and supplies of answering machines. There is a variety of units available that can be adapted for this use. Target homes as the market and sell via direct mail and telephone follow-up. There is a great deal of potential for successfully selling this product as such a large market exists.

Now if there's no one home, leave a message:

> "Courier service was here at 2:00 p.m. with a parcel. Please phone 777-7777."
> "This is Aunt Sally. I'm in town and will call back later."

Possible Name: Door Talker

Hanging Tree

Did you know that fruit ripens more quickly when hung than when stored in a bowl? Design a fruit tree!

Attach a solid tree branch or a uniquely-shaped piece of wood to a base. Design so that fruit can be hung from the fruit tree. This will decorate the kitchen, and will be a conversation piece.

Sell to fruit buyers at grocery stores and fruit stands. Package attractively in clear plastic wrap. Include an illustration.

Parking Meter Pay Idea

Select a designated area as a route and patrol parking meters. When a meter has expired, fill it with change and place a pre-printed notice under the windshield wiper. The notice could be worded as follows:

> "Today we plugged your expired or nearly-expired meter. By doing this the possibility of a parking fine or of having your automobile towed has been avoided. Our business is to patrol parking meters and to ensure that you are able to save embarrassment and money.
>
> Please mail $4.00 to the undersigned. This is the fee for our service and funds deposited in the meter, versus approximately $20.00 in fines. Of course this is not mandatory. Please be assured that we will continue to support your interests in the future and have noted your license number in the event that you choose to take advantage of our service. Thank you very much for your anticipated positive reaction to our business service venture."

This is a unique and interesting venture. Auto owners would no longer have to rush from important meetings or from shopping to fill parking meters.

Create a fashion statement for cyclists.

Make wrist bracelets from bicycle chains and plastic coat them in a variety of colors. Attach an encased message, to be worn with the bracelet, ie.: for a red bracelet:

"I have a red bike. Cycling is fast, fun and healthy."

Use a variety of sayings so shoppers can select one to suit them. Illustrations would be great as well. Chain bracelets should be attractive and symbolize that the wearer is active and proud of the sport. This is also a great new way to begin conversations.

The potential for this item is tremendous! Fashion accessory items are limited for cyclists and people are cycling in record numbers. Gold trim or gems would dress up the bracelets for the more sophisticated cyclists!

This chain bracelet fad is a sure link to profit!

Some don't hear opportunity knock because they're too busy knocking opportunity.

New Neighbor Video

Are you a video camera buff? How about making some money at your hobby? Residents in a new city require services and information about their new community.

Put together a video on your city, its history, people, resources, attractions and services. Politicians, television and radio personalities could give a big "Welcome home" on video. Approach businesses and present a plan showing reasons for them to advertise in the video. Include statistics to show the number of new arrivals and comparable costs for clients to use other advertising mediums.

Potential clients include law firms, accountants, auto repair shops, banks, hair stylists, health clubs, sports clubs and food stores. They may wish to include discount coupons for new residents.

Provide the video free-of-charge to the welcoming or greeting service in your community. Update information, renew and add contracts for advertising every four to six months.

Get the picture?

Money talks, but you have to turn up the volume.

Business Card Extra

People in the sales industry are always looking for ways to improve their earnings. This idea does that and also provides relevant information for their customers.

Select and match the company's products and sales people via their business cards, ie.: a realtor in residential sales is always with potential home buyers and gives out many business cards. Match a furniture store with the realtor. Print a message on the back of the realtor's business card. Something like, "Discount available with this card" will encourage shopping at the furniture store. Sales resulting from business cards will be monitored so that the realtor can receive a fee. The realtor makes additional income while enhancing the saleability of a house, ie.: "There's a chair in the store that would just make this room!" The purchaser is well treated and the furniture company is successfully promoting its business to qualified prospects. The realtor is not necessarily the only match for the business cards of the furniture company. Match a finance company to the furniture company and put the realtor on the back of a mortgage company card.

Establish a "select and match" company. Sell memberships, charge monthly fees and receive a commission from the printer doing the business cards.

Describe the program in a brochure to sell memberships. Record clients' business information so this can be matched with others. A fee of $150.00 plus a monthly charge of $25.00 is reasonable. Many, many memberships can be

(Continued on page 80)

Business Card Extra (continued)

sold! Match the cards and have them approved by both clients. Monitor the cross-merchandising and replace or exchange card partners as required.

Possible Names: Dual Performance
                   Two Time Sales
                   Double Card Sales

When summer arrives, thousands of us take to the outdoors!

Invest in durable inflatable plastic chairs which can be sold or rented during numerous outdoor events. These include air shows, music festivals, beach activities and auction sales.

Include a small pump with the chairs or have some device available to fill the chairs quickly with air.

Sell advertising and have these messages screened on the chairs. There is a big demand for this product and service.

Nature provides every bird its food but does not throw it into the nest.

Phone Care Line

Establish a service for calling and checking in on teenagers while their parents are working or away. Your service could also include calling on the elderly or others who live on their own.

This service can provide security, relief, and assistance if it becomes necessary. Parents are not always able to call home while they are working. Others who have aging parents often live far from them and would like assurances that their loved ones are being routinely checked.

Clearly outline the services you provide. Include a "hot-line" so that you can be reached in case of emergency. This business can be run from the home with virtually no overhead. You can offer occasional services for an hourly or daily rate, or monthly services for which clients prepay.

Possible Names: Phone Care Service
                   All Distance Phone Service

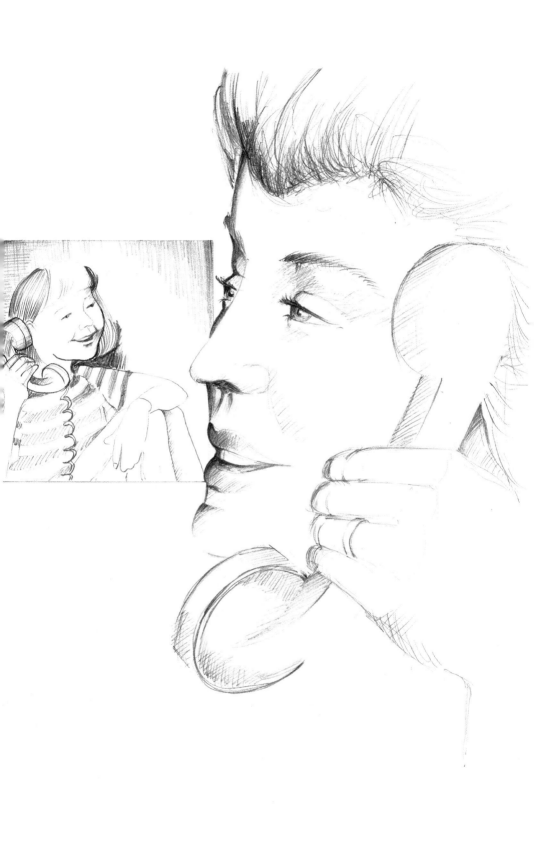

Computer Store Directory

How often do you run into a large grocery store or wholesale warehouse for something specific only to chase up and down aisles looking for it? Ever tried to find an employee to ask? No more frustration for shoppers!

Develop a computer program that can provide the location and availability of items carried in the store. Shoppers would go to the computer directory, make their enquiry and continue shopping "with direction." A computer directory would not only provide customer service but also would free employees from giving directions.

Present your computer program to grocery stores and other large retail outlets. As part of your sales package include teaching employees who can then update the directory as changes occur. Provide your clients with a phone number to call should they require further assistance with the computer program.

Funny Money

An enterprising university posted a sign that read "education is to business what fertilizer is to farming."

Taxi Cab Confection Sales

Millions of passengers ride in the rear seats of taxis while being driven to their destination. Many would buy gum, mints or candy if these were available. Sunglasses, toiletries and key chains are also potential sales items.

Design a clear plastic holder to fit over the back of the front car seat. Display several items in the holder with the prices clearly marked. The holder should be sealed for control and the driver would sell the requested items to the customer. Also design an inventory case. Market direct to taxi drivers.

This is a terrific opportunity for anyone! The taxi's income is supplemented, the passengers can "mini shop," and you sell plastic holders. Consider supplying confectionary items to the now thousands of taxi type stores. Contact wholesalers for candy and other items. This idea is worth the ride!

Possible Name: Cab Confection
                   Taxi Store

Stilts

A tall idea! Re-introduce a children's product from long ago. Although still used by some, stilts are seldom available at retail outlets.

Buy lumber, 1"x2" or 2"x2" and about 5' to 8' long. Attach foot blocks from a 2"x4" with screws or nails. Design the stilts so that the footholds can be adjusted up or down to change the height from the ground. Make them in a variety of lengths and colors and put together with a fashionable carrying tote. Attach a card to the stilts which explains how to use them. Also include an interesting history.

Research the market for a suitable retail price. Then approach sports outlets, department and toy stores and present your new product.

Success is easy... just get up one more time than you fall.

We cherish our photos and the memories they provide. Too often, however, disaster strikes and photos are gone forever.

Offer a service to store photograph negatives. The service is to include having negatives picked up every so often, dated and itemized. The negatives need to be stored in fireproof and water resistant containers.

Approach camera and film stores to advertise your service.

Design a brochure with illustrations and testimonials from insurance companies and individuals. Establish a price structure and get going!

Possible Names: Photo Copy
                     Get the Picture?

Millions of people are employed but how many people are working?

This idea is great for a home business. Create a form-fitting style of hat and target the sports market for sales. This product is ideal for runners, beach volleyball players and tennis players. The young people will love this new gypsy look!

Use a rectangular cotton fabric, approximately 26" wide and 17" long. Each end is to be open. Use elastic, as well as a drawstring and lace lock at one end and hem the other. Slip the elasticized end over your head. Flip the other open end down under the drawstring and pull the lace lock tight. Voila! One "cool" hat!

Use a variety of fabric and lace colors. Distribute to sports and department stores for sale and get ready for more orders!

Possible Names: Sack Hat
                    Pirates Cap

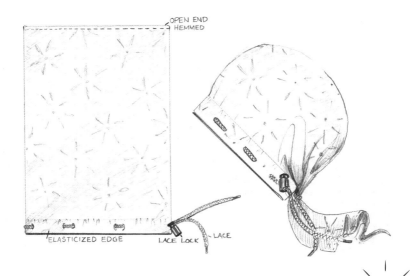

For decades people have been renting storage space to hold their boats, cars, R.V.'s, bikes, sports equipment, business and household items. Here is a new "development" in the billion dollar self-storage industry – buying storage space. Self-storage tenants, businesses and individuals can now own their own garage.

Concept: Condominiumise storage units and offer individual ownership in the ultimate storage concept with the option for either rental income or capital gains. Develop or convert existing self-storage units to condos.

Market: This idea is for large cities, small towns and resort areas. Potential owners include:

• Professionals (doctors, lawyers, accountants) – to store records.
• Retail stores – to store excess inventory, display and promotional materials, new stock, etc.
• Distributors – to provide mini-warehousing for their products enroute from factories to retailers.
• Service companies – to store materials and equipment, company vehicles.
• Restaurants – to store excess furniture, table linen, wines, etc.
• Seasonal retailers (ski shops, sports rentals, windsurfer outlets) – to store out-of-season stock.

(Continued on next page)

95

• Radio stations – to store records and tapes.
• Others – to store R.V.'s, campers, trailers, cars, motorcycles, boats, snowmobiles, windsurfers, skis, camping gear, bikes, golf equipment, etc.
• Condo dweller – to provide a workshop or storage area.
• Investors – for revenue and capital gain.

Plan and
Design:

Secure a property suitable for this project. Hire an architect to prepare a site plan and to design the project. Some general information and options are:

• Storage Conversion: Obtain an existing facility. Ensure that the fire, building and electric codes can be met with reasonable cost. Review the mix of unit sizes and research the market. Inspect the tenant list for potential purchasers and long term tenants for investment owners.
• Develop Property: It's best to have the proper zoning for the site to avoid the cost and time to rezone. The property should be well located with good access and frontage. About half of the site area can be built on, ie.: one acre of land will provide about 22,000 square feet of saleable storage space or approximately 100 condominium titles.

Construction:
- Buildings: Wood frame, concrete or block construction. Concrete is fast, requires less labor and can be used for walls and ceilings, to create a secure vault type storage unit. Concrete should be 3", 4", or 5" depending on the size of the unit.
- Floors: concrete slab.
- Doors: Steel roll-up. Consider "people doors" as part of the roll-up door. This allows the owner access without having to lift the large door.
- Roofing: Asphalt shingles.
- Paving: Asphalt.
- Fencing: High perimeter fencing.
- Security: Install a security system with individual codes to access the gate. Door alarms for each unit and an on-site manager are also possibilities.
- Lighting: Exterior and interior.
- Options: Provide power, heat or air-conditioning on request.

Unit Sizes: Design each unit with the same width and offer up to five increments in length. For example:

    12' x 10'
    12' x 20'
    12' x 30'
    12' x 40'
    12' x 50'

Ceiling height can be 10 feet and increased to

(Continued next page)

16 feet for the 40 and 50 foot lengths, to accommodate R.V.'s and mezzanines.

Marketing: This is a new and specialized field and is best marketed by the developer. Work with realtors and offer a referral fee. Develop brochures and a working model for display in malls and at trade shows. Hire professional sales people and offer an attractive sales plan. Begin sales before construction.

Potential: This concept has incredible potential! A pro-forma is shown below.
Construction and Sales Costs:

Land cost – (1 acre, zoned industrial)	= $150,000
Concrete Buildings (formed and erected) @ $12.00 per sq. ft. for 22,000 ft.	= $264,000
Paving, fencing, security, roofing, floors, electrical, doors, etc. @ $12.00 per sq. ft.	= $264,000
Management, legals, design, contingency	= $100,000
Sale Costs (commissions)	= $125,000
Advertising, brochures	= $ 25,000
Cost of financing (based on 6 months @ 10% of construction costs of $778,000)	= $ 38,900
Total Project Cost	= $966,900

(Continued on page 100)

Sales:

22,000 sq. ft. @ $65.00 per ft.
average price   = $1,430,000

Net Profit before taxes   = $463,100
1) If a unit was rented at present market rental rates, the sale prices would earn a return on investment sufficient to justify the price.
2) The time frame to develop and market one acre is about six months.

Summary: This is truly a "bright idea" and can be done in any size community. A new way of doing an old thing!

Possible Names: Your Storage Condos
Warehouse and Storage Condos

Excellence is to do a common thing in an uncommon way.

Craft Agent

This idea is crafty! So many people make craft items, ie.: earrings, pillow covers, quilts, clothing, etc. Generally, crafts are not well distributed. Consumers are often unaware of certain items and where they can get them. Become an agent for craft makers.

Provide a service to include product consulting, pricing and distribution. Catalog your client's products and approach stores for orders. Organize flea market and garage sales for clients. Charge an initial fee of $100.00 to assist in your costs and also charge a sales commission. This can range from 10-30% and should apply to all sales. In addition, publish a "Craft Book" for advertising. Distribute the book free-of-charge. Charge clients for the space used in the book. Consider selling advertising to other businesses as well. A forty or fifty page book will be fun to read and will create active sales.

Cheermitts

Clap your hands or wave a banner! Now you can do both together!

Product:
Cheermitts are discs which can be strapped to each hand and have messages screened on them. Cheermitts can be made from neoprene which is a firm plastic foam that is washable and durable. This material also makes a loud, slapping sound when hit together, perfect for thunderous applause at a sports event!

Market:
All sports events including professional basketball, football, baseball and hockey. College sports, minor league and junior teams in all events are part of this extremely large market. Hundreds of thousands of fans participate in encouraging sports teams every day. Cheermitts can also be promoted for use at concerts and political rallies.

Marketing and
Distribution Plan:
• Sell via conventional outlets such as sporting goods stores, drugstores, discount stores, and in arena or stadium concessions.
• Sell direct before or during an event.
• Sell advertising to a sponsor and distribute Cheermitts free or at a reduced

charge. For example, if a cola company was the advertiser on Cheermitts and gave them away to fans, they would benefit through increased sales of their product. The cola name and logo would be seen by every fan and would receive coverage on radio and television. Potential advertisers include automotive dealerships, food stores, sports and beverage companies.

Potential: The Cheermitts concept could command a profit in any area and in virtually all sports events. If done nationally, with a professional sports league, this idea has the potential of earning millions of dollars.

This bright business idea deserves a hand!

Possible Names: Cheermitts
Cheer Gloves
Happy Hands

TRIUMPH: "UMPH" added to try.

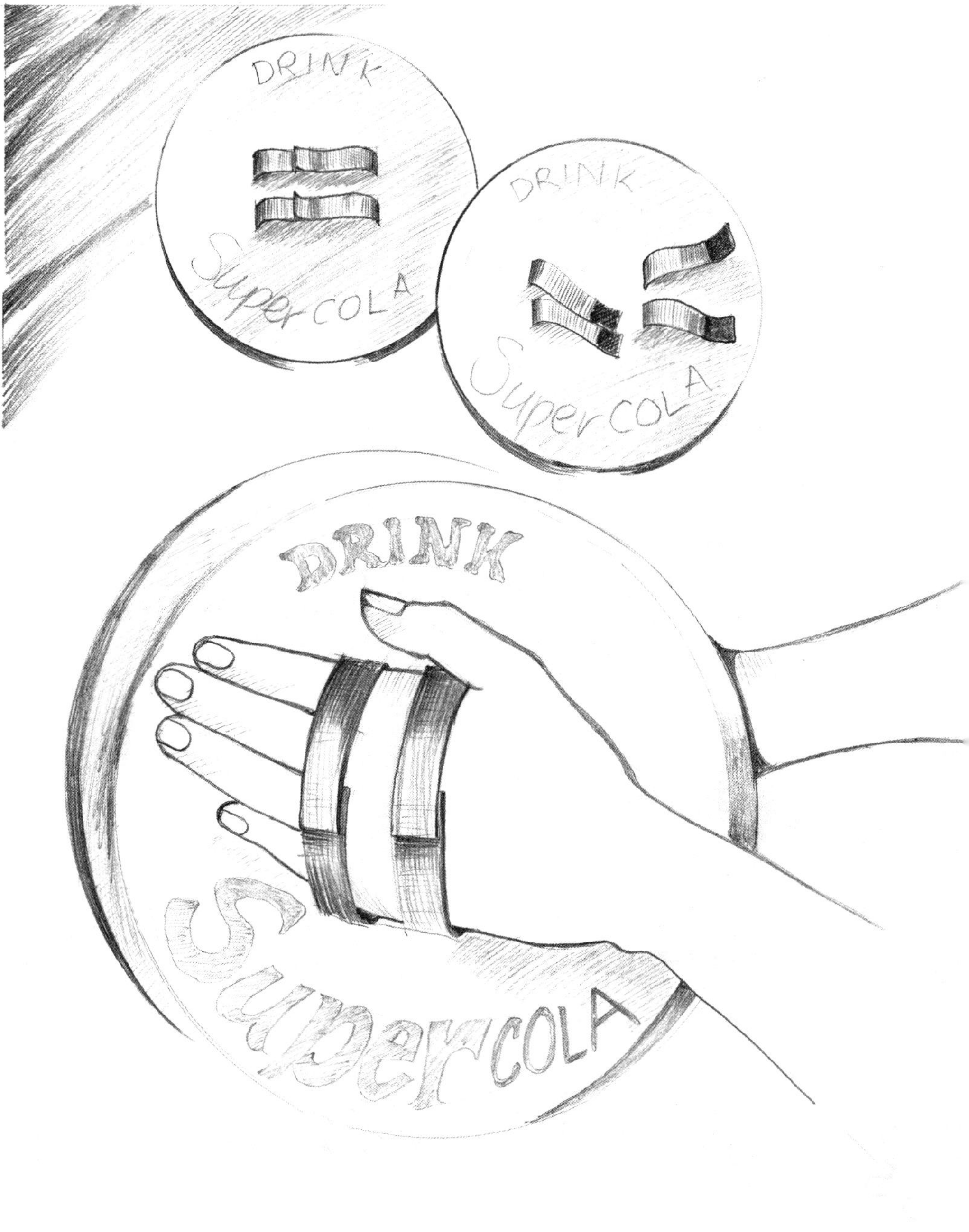
DRINK
Super COLA
DRINK
Super COLA
DRINK
Super COLA

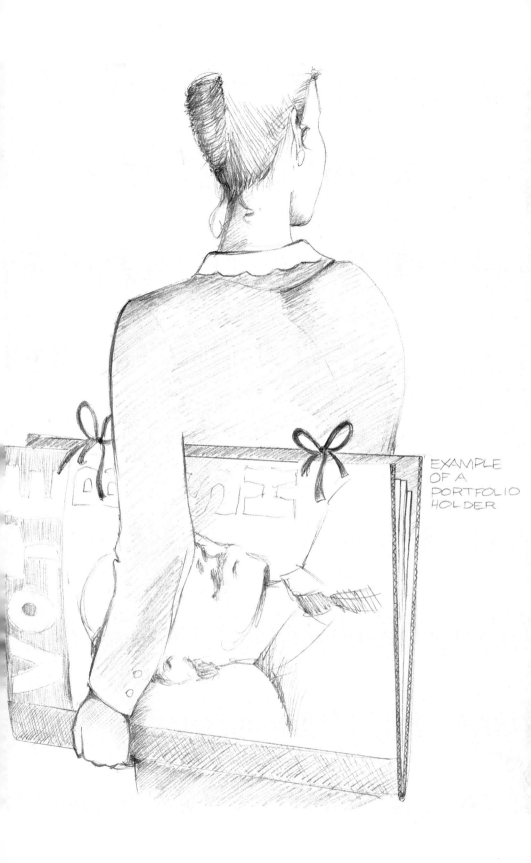

EXAMPLE
OF A
PORTFOLIO
HOLDER

How about recycling political campaign signs into designer briefcases and portfolio holders?

Corrugated plastic is often used for election signs and is expensive. The design work and colors are already paid for and the signs can often be obtained at no cost. Get advice on designing and manufacturing the briefcases from a printer or box manufacturer. Not only will the briefcases be durable and practical, they also have collector value, depending on the name and significance of the candidate or party.

Contact politicians for permission to use the sign and offer to pick them up after an election. Other signs that can be used are beverage and food product signs. Sale prices will vary depending on the popularity of the sign. Retail prices should range from $20.00 - $50.00 for briefcases. Research retail prices for portfolio holders and file folders, as well.

Present to office supply companies, department stores and novelty shops. This idea can make a lot of money... and keeps old signs out of the landfills.

The public will vote for this idea!

Postage Machine

Many businesses lease a postage meter. These are compact, simple to use, and they organize the company's mail system. The postage meter however, is expensive.

Have an engineer design a postage machine that can be filled with regular stamps (versus an electronically-metered stamp machine) and sell the machine direct to the user, versus leasing it. The economics should be easy to justify. Items to be included in the postage machine are: a postal rate schedule, several stamp denominations and a moistener for the stamps and envelopes. Also include a return address stamp in the machine's design.

The market for this item is huge! A business and some homes need an organized kit for their postage… at a reasonable price! Market to office supply firms and stationery shops and also by direct sales to small businesses.

Some people dream of worthy accomplishments while others stay awake and do them.

LOCAL
OVERSEAS
200 G
300 G
400 G
500 G
700 G
800 G
900 G
Terrace View Estates
10351 North Road

Timely Investment

Each year there are numerous items produced which will be valuable in the future. Few are saved however. How much is an original sealed Elvis Presley album worth today? Or a sealed magazine from long ago?

The idea is to design and market a storage case for collecting certain items. The case should be durable and fire and water resistant. Divide the storage case into several compartments. These can be labeled and used for specific years. People would collect certain things and store them in the appropriate year compartment. Provide a list of items with income potential, ie.: wines, electronic items, coins, fad or trendy products, recordings, sports cards, newspapers and magazines. Include a system to record dates and inventory. The storage case organizes and secures the collection for enjoyment and investment.

Present to gift shops and department stores. This product is unique and should command good sales and profit.

Possible Names: Back to the Future
                   Time Savings

If you don't learn anything from your mistakes, there's no sense in making them.

Fashion Helmet

Now you can be fashionably protected! Design and market a variety of helmet styles: Cowboy hat, civil war hat, ball cap, etc. Another idea is a helmet cover. This can be made of nylon and spandex with elastic around the bottom. The cover can be stretched over a helmet for a new look. Attach accessories to a variety of cover shapes and styles.

For price quotations and advice, contact helmet manufacturers and present the designs that you require. A clothing manufacturer can provide a price for helmet covers. Sell to sport and department stores.

This idea is fun and encourages people to wear helmets.

Possible Names: Fashion Helmets
                      Helmet Hat
                      Hard Head

Smart Money

If it were not for optimists, the pessimist would never know how happy they aren't.

Follow the crowd! This idea works driving down the road or while parked at golf courses, music festivals, conventions or sports events.

Install an oversized screen on the side of a truck box to be used to show videos. Include a soundtrack. Advertisers can become part of a hard-hitting and unique advertising program. Consider allowing clients to sell their product from the back of the truck while the video is being played, ie.: the video could show an orchardist picking apples and they would sell apples from the truck.

Potential customers include beverage companies, sports outlets, direct-sales producers, etc. Let's get this show on the road!

Possible Names: Traveling Show
                   Have Ad Will Travel

Talk is cheap..... but not at an auction!

Idea Consulting Sales Agent

People with business ideas have many questions. For example: "What is a patent?" "Do I need to patent my idea?" "What is the cost?" "Should I trademark my concept?" "Who can I confide in about my idea?" "Should I hire a sales company or create my own?" "How do I get financing?"

Form a consulting company to specialize in business ideas. Develop a system to satisfy the needs of the client. Discuss their ideas and help to expand and develop them. Access government incentives and programs. Arrange for legal and accounting advice. Enter into a confidentiality agreement with each client. Charge an up-front fee plus an hourly rate. Advertise in newspapers and entrepreneur magazines.

A bright business idea!

You can't teach a salesman anything, only remind him of what he already knows.

Employees are often too busy to deal with the image that is being created by their company. It's sometimes difficult for them to confront certain issues and to be aware of others.

Establish a service company to work with a firm's employees. Focus would be on appearance, mannerisms and friendliness of employees. They are the representatives of the employer and must treat people like they, themselves would like to be treated. They must dress and groom well. In addition, employees must be proud of their work and of the company they work for. An independent service company can work with employees in these areas more effectively than an employer.

Develop motivational seminars and encourage communication with management. Morale will soar and so will productivity and profit!

Funny Money

The quickest way to double your money is to fold it over once and put it in your pocket.

Pine Cone Fire Idea

Need extra money? Here's a sure-fire idea. Pine cones burn easily and have an attractive colored flame. Collect truckloads of cones, bag and sell them.

Package the cones (about two dozen) in netting and attach a printed card with details about their use. Another idea is to pack two or three cones in a brown paper bag that is pre-stamped or printed on. Something like, "Cone fire starter," and "Place bag on grate and light," would be effective.

Price at $1.00 to $3.00 per bag and sell hundreds of bags per day! Sell direct from the roadside, at flea markets, door-to-door and to lumber yards and gas stations for resale. The initial costs are very low and overhead is virtually non-existent. Consumers will enjoy the variety for their fireplace.

This is an ideal business for students or as a part-time venture for anyone.

A "hot" way to make money!

Beard Trim Tray

A man can leave a mess when he trims his beard or moustache. This idea will eliminate the difficult and irritating task of cleaning up after a "face trim."

Meet with an engineer and plastic company to design a product that can fit securely while trimming. It should be molded plastic and horse-shoe shaped to fit the neck. Use velcro to secure the tray around the neck. The design should include a brace for a better fit which could also be used to empty the tray into a waste basket.

Package in clear wrap. Include an illustration showing its use. Consider including scissors and face lotion. Photos of beard and moustache styles from other eras would be interesting.

This idea is sure to clean up!

Possible Names: Trim Bin
                    Face Trim Kit

Mobile Book Sales

Design and build a mobile book cart. Stock a good selection of titles. These can include romance, mystery, business and western novels.

People who read during their work or lunch breaks are always interested in getting books. Take the store to them!

Direct your book sales to office workers. Establish a route and attend it regularly. Hot dog or popcorn vendors are usually well positioned so look for them to determine higher traffic areas. New books can be acquired from a wholesaler or you may consider working with an established book store. Secondhand books would work well too and could sell for considerably less. Auction sales and used book stores are good sources for these. Offer trade-ins to encourage repeat business. This also provides an excellent way to rotate inventory.

Manage only one cart or hire others and have several. Consider selling the carts and stocking the book inventory for each cart owner.

Possible Names: Traveling Book Sales
                    Reading Cart

Movers Group

Independent furniture and freight movers don't advertise as much as they would like. Often their exposure is restricted to the yellow pages in the phone book. Small advertising budgets make it difficult to compete with large movers and truck rental firms.

Organize a movers group! Offer an operations structure for promotion that each independent can benefit from. Prepare and place advertisements for the Moving Group. Promote the Moving Group and the trucking industry with publicity as well. Focus advertising on the advantages of using a movers group member, ie.: "Support small business for better service from owner operators for less money." Provide training for consistent service and standards. Obtain group medical benefits and special insurance packages. Consider supplying legal and accounting advice as part of the benefit package. Organize bulk purchases of tires, oil and truck parts for members. Introduce a logo and colors for clothing and trucks. Use the group name for all promotions, ie.: "Mike's Moving, a Moving Group Member... each mover, independently owned."

Have an attorney prepare contracts. Set a fee for joining the Moving Group and charge a percentage based on sales – 5-10% is reasonable.

There is safety in numbers! As a group, trucking companies will now have a loud voice. Target firms with one to twenty trucks. Productivity and profits will increase for movers and the Moving Group will be rewarded too!

Designer Paper Clip

Paper clips are already a well-accepted and successful product. There is still room, however, for a new idea in this market.

Design and market paper clips of various shapes and styles. Appeal to students as well as businesses for sales. Package a variety of designer paper clips in each container. These can include corporate names and logos, dollar signs, astrology signs and animals. Present to office supply and stationery stores.

Honey Novelty Sales

This is a sweet idea!

Sell honey in your own design of squeeze bottles that are fun and unique, ie.: put a cowboy hat and chaps on a bottle of honey and label it, "My Texas Honey," or label a hula dancer, "My Hawaiian Honey." Attach a card with a greeting such as, "Give me a squeeze!" or, "You're sweet!"

Honey producers will provide the product for your custom made containers.

Prepare flyers for retailers or present to a food broker or distributor. Markets include food stores, flea markets and gift shops.

Make Money honey!

Message Band

Often notepaper is attached to pages that have been clipped together for filing. This idea eliminates the need for a paper clip and provides space for messages.

Have a self-adhesive strip attached to each end of note-paper. Up to twenty-five of these can be attached to one another and sold as message pads. Each sheet can be removed and folded over pages to bind or hold them to-gether. Messages can be written on either side of the notepaper, ie.: "file these under the Jones deal" or "please type and mail."

Ask for price quotations from two or more printers. Describe the use on the underside of the message pad with an illus-tration. Have samples made.

Prepare a brochure and solicit orders, direct, or contact office supply distributors. Potential customers include schools, bookstores, office supply companies and stationery shops. This item is a perfect addition to an existing product line or as an individual item for a start-up venture.

It's sticky business!

If you never make a mistake, you may go through life unnoticed.

This is the information age!

Students, business people and others often require information for research, reports or presentations. Establish a phone-in service that can locate requested information or provide assistance in particular subject areas.

This is a viable opportunity for those who have access to computer encyclopedias, library computer networks, reference books and other information sources.

Prepare a brochure outlining the kinds of information and assistance your service provides. Give examples of questions, ie.: How many sheep are there in the world? How many pages was George Washington's will and what was the size of his estate?

Advertise at colleges, high schools, and the local newspaper. Obtain a 1-900 user pay service number and charge up to $1.25 per minute.

Opportunity is calling!

Pavement Message

This is a unique welcome mat... in cement! Use the pavement in front of businesses for advertising. Something like, "Welcome to John's Bakery!" would be great engraved in the cement at the door to the bakery, or "Welcome to the Jone's," would be attractive at home.

Get approval from the city for this new idea.

Contact a concrete company for help in cutting out portions of the sidewalks and for pouring new cement. Design wooden forms for the slogans to be pressed into the new cement.

Charge the client for the cement and for the advertising message. This is a solid idea!

No Auto Spill

Have you ever had a cup of coffee in a car holder when a sudden turn caused it to spill? Here's an idea!

Have an engineer design a cup holder that moves against the direction of the car. A free-moving weight in the holder will allow this reaction. When the car turns right the cup of coffee will lean to the left and the contents will stay level, even though everything else in the car is moving to the right.

Package with illustrations and market to auto supply shops and hardware stores.

High Rise Floor Condo

Many corporations would like to own their own downtown office but often the cost is prohibitive. Here's a bright idea.

Condominiumise each floor of a high rise building and sell to existing tenants and others. Look for a building with a strong tenant mix. Secure the property with a conditional agreement. Prepare an in-depth business plan and present to sophisticated investors for financing. Include detailed drawings from an architect and a list of prospective purchasers.

Prepare pricing and brochures for tenants and approach them to purchase a floor of the building. Sales will be subject to receiving condominium approval from the city. Consult with an attorney and have documents prepared.

Condo purchasers can now invest in prime property and no longer have to pay rent.

Benjamin Franklin discovered electricity but the person who invented the meter made all the money.

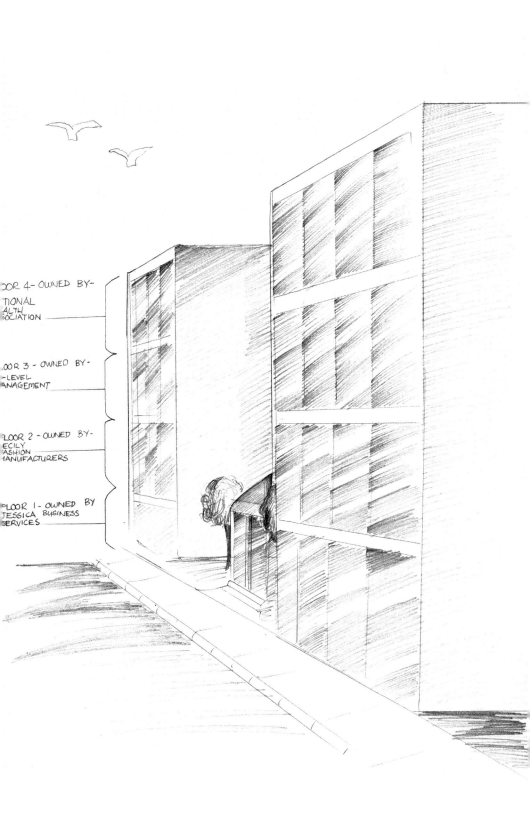

OOR 4 - OWNED BY-
TIONAL
ALTH
OCIATION

OOR 3 - OWNED BY-
-LEVEL
ANAGEMENT

FLOOR 2 - OWNED BY-
ECILY
ASHION
MANUFACTURERS

FLOOR 1 - OWNED BY
JESSICA BUSINESS
SERVICES

Umbrella Plate

Juice "squirts everywhere!" when a grapefruit is eaten. Design a plate for grapefruit eaters with a miniature umbrella on the side. This is a fun idea and can be marketed to grapefruit growers for a promotional item and to grocery stores.

Chimney Sweep

Here's a clean idea! Develop a home kit for cleaning chimneys.

Contact fireplace companies to inquire about equipment that will be needed. Assemble what's needed in an attractive kit and include instructions on how to clean a chimney. Ask the fireplace company for a list of client's names for leads. Also contact insurance companies, building contractors and apartment owners for leads. Dress in an Olde England Chimney Sweep outfit and contact potential purchasers.

Valet Grocery Cart Parking

Many grocery stores and supermarkets have a coin system for grocery carts where a quarter is needed to rent the cart for shopping. Contact the store manager to present the idea of parking carts for customers. A location by the entrance and exit doors is needed. Have a podium or bell captain type stand with signs. Have the valet person dress in a red tuxedo with a top hat. Advertise that you will return the cart for the quarter deposit. Give a portion of this to a charity to encourage use. Consider helping unload the carts as an additional incentive for the shoppers to have their cart parked. The grocery store benefits because the valet attendants act as store greeters. They also could thank each shopper as they leave. In addition, the valet company should have a large sign thanking the store for supporting them in their free enterprise endeavor.

Research the traffic flow for peak times. There may be times when it is considered best to not attend the booth based on slow traffic. Advise the store before this happens. Possibly the store would be interested in paying for these services, versus doing without.

This is a bright idea for students to either do themselves or for someone to establish cart parking outlets at several stores and to hire students. Remuneration should be via a percentage of sales.

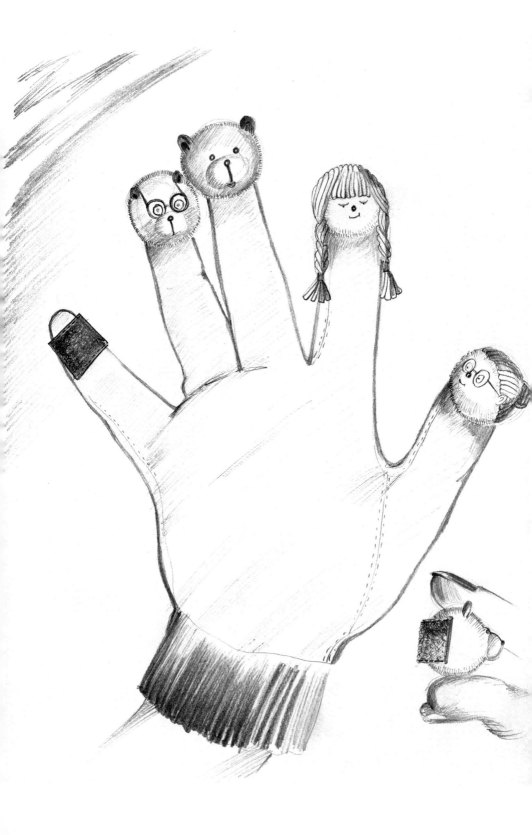

Children enjoy a good story... now provide a show too!

Obtain or sew story gloves. Design faces and characters which can be attached to the fingers with velcro. Provide stories to accompany the characters and your idea is ready to be packaged for market.

Story gloves may be sold at craft shows or flea markets. If you arrange mass production, markets include nurseries, daycare centers and toy stores.

He needs a bright business idea... he's so poor he can't afford to pay attention.

Briefcase Billboard

This idea is sure to create conversation. Design a clear plastic briefcase cover to hold brochures, business cards or advertising. Visualize an airplane full of business people traveling a long distance. If a realtor had a brochure displayed in the plastic cover of a case, ie.: "For sale, warehouse in Phoenix, Arizona," other passengers would notice and an inquiry could result in a sale. Other examples include, "My company is in oil and trades on the NYSE and the TSE," and, "Executive cars for sale. Ask me, I sell cars!"

This is like having a big business card or a billboard! This opens the way for personal interaction and increased business. Many business people have a use for this type of exposure.

Market the briefcase covers by mail order and to office supply companies.

Possible Names: Communicase
                   Billboard Holder

Invoice and Service Control Agent

This idea is best described by comparison. If you hire a painter to paint your home, terms of agreement are negotiated and you can see the quality of the work as it progresses. The invoice is produced when the job is completed and there are no surprises. If the terms of the agreement are not met, you can withhold payment until the work is done to your satisfaction.

Invoices from professionals (lawyers, accountants, etc.) however, are quite different. These bills seldom indicate the hours worked and they are often higher than expected. Clients usually receive a bill with no break down of services. It simply states, "Fee For Services," and an amount. Unlike the painter, professional services are mostly intangible and therefore difficult to match results with cost.

This idea is to establish an Invoice Control Company to be the agent for the accountant or law client. The agent would negotiate fees, review services and approve all invoices. Additional services include selecting a lawyer or accountant, negotiating the hourly rate, monitoring their ability and use of time, and negotiating settlements with the other parties.

Design a kit that includes various methods for comparing and monitoring these professional services. One possibility is an earnings test, ie.: How many hours did the professional work on a day for which the client was billed for three hours work? If eight, then multiply this by the hourly rate. This total should equal the billings for the entire day. If the billings are more than eight hours, more than one client is being charged for the same time.

140

Prepare an elaborate brochure and distribute to potential clients. Use phrases like: "An employer (client) has the right to command exclusivity of billed time and satisfactory work from an employee (lawyer, accountant, etc.), "Any reluctance from a firm of professionals, to cooperate with an invoice control agent should be viewed suspiciously," or, "We will ensure that at all times, you know what you owe."

Sell memberships to businesses and charge a fee per file or hour. This idea can be profitable and also provides a savings of money and stress to the client.

Possible Names: Columbo Control
                    Pro-Fee Agent

A will of your own is not as good as the will of a rich relative.

No showers, or long lines for cold showers, are an unfortunate reality at many cycling or running events. Spray away grit in a traveling shower! Design up to fourteen shower stalls for a tandem truck trailer. Include private dressing rooms. Chairs and benches can be secured to the floor. A special hot water tank can be built to provide the hot water. Consult an engineer on designs for all water requirements.

Contact running, cycling and track clubs for event schedules. Some races attract thousands of participants. Travel to selected events. Charge one or two dollars per shower.

Obtain a sponsor. Contact running shoe companies, beverage and sports companies. This is an exciting opportunity for advertisers. Their message is targeted to a select group and is highly visible while being driven to other events.

Consider selling juice, fruit and sports items from the truck during an event. This would complement the venture as well as being a supplement to income.

Board Game

Board games are fun and popular! Design and develop a board game based on general knowledge.

Suggested layout: Select a board size and have it made with laminated cardboard. Randomly list and circle each letter of the alphabet on the board, also list five columns of topics, ie.: cities, countries, cars, fruits and vegetables and plants or flowers. Provide notepaper and pencils with the game.

Suggested rules for the game: There's no limit to the number of players. Each player has a turn and is to close their eyes and place a finger inside the circle of a letter. This player then asks the others to secretly write names for each category beginning with the chosen letter. The one who selects the letter is the judge for that round. Five points are awarded for the name if used by more than one player and ten points are awarded if the name is chosen by one player only. This encourages players to be original and creative!

This game is inexpensive to produce. Package in bright colors with illustrations. Market to game and toy stores.

Possible Names: Board of Knowledge
                   Bright Board

Auto Television Network

Many cable television networks have one channel designated to car and truck sales. Photos are shown with a price and telephone number. Although somewhat effective, this is dull and lacks action.

Create television ads of vehicles. Have the owner or salesperson walk around the car while explaining various features. At the same time, the price, telephone number and location of the car could be shown on the screen.

Prepare a business proposal with illustrations to present to the cable companies. Negotiate a price and terms for the exclusive use of the auto trader channel. Prepare pricing and statistics for potential customers. Approach car salespeople to buy advertising space. They could ask for financial support from the car dealer and for the cost of the ads.

Hire a fun show host to introduce those selling the cars and trucks. The host would also be able entertain viewers, ie.: "The third caller gets a free case of motor oil, a car wash, etc." Promotional items can be obtained at no cost from companies who would enjoy the publicity. Consider selling commercials as well. The idea is to make this venture a television program versus only a sales service. A specialized and professional program of this nature is long overdue!

Possible Names: C.A.T. Network (Car And Truck)
                   T.V. Auto Program

Tire Use

Old and worn-out tires are bad for the environment. Here's a way to recycle tires!

Convert tires to sand boxes, floor mats, flower pots, apartment garden plots, boat docks or feeders for livestock. Chain two-inch tire strips together to make floor mats, or cut tires in half for a variety of other uses. Market to lumber yards, hardware stores and marine sales outlets.

Possible Names: Big Tread Sales
                      Last Mile Service

Barrel of Fun

Create an adult "surprise barrel." Seal various items in a plastic or wooden barrel. Include peanuts, games, books, etc. Point out the uses for the barrel when it's empty, ie.: a stool, table or toy bin.

Sell the barrel and the mystery! Retail for under $20.00 and target adults for your market. Sell to gift shops and department stores.

To trade an item or service for another is a proven way to do business. Have a monthly publication produced, listing items available for barter, ie.: "Plumber will provide up to $500.00 worth of work for the same value of car tires," "Accountant will exchange services for office renovations or sports equipment," "Radio station will trade advertising space for a new fax machine."

Sell the advertising space for barter goods. Contact all types of businesses and create barter from their business, ie.: suggest trading products or services for other items normally required in their business.

Explain the advantages of this system in a brochure. These include: no sales commissions, increased sales at full retail value, no cash required for purchases, etc.

Initially distribute the magazine at no cost to encourage readership.

Possible Names: Barter Trader
                   Barter Book

Your Own Bright Idea

Your Own Bright Idea

Your Own Bright Idea

Your Own Bright Idea

Your Own Bright Idea

The author is available for business consulting and speaking engagements. If your organization, business or club would like more information, please include the name, phone and fax number of the contact person below with a brief outline of your interest to:

Bright Publishing Inc.
Box 24002, Lakefront P.O.
Kelowna, British Columbia
Canada V1Y 9P9

Bright Publishing Inc.
Room 261, Box 5000
Oroville, Washington
U.S.A. 98844

_____

_____

_____

_____

_____

_____

_____

Any Bright Business Idea or money joke that you wish to share can be mailed to Bright Publishing Inc. at either of the above addresses.

If these are new to the publisher and used in future Bright Business Ideas publications, special acknowledgement will be given.

Bright Business Ideas

Bright Publishing Inc.
Box 24002, Lakefront P.O.
Kelowna, British Columbia
Canada V1Y 9P9

Bright Publishing Inc.
Room 261, Box 5000
Oroville, Washington
U.S.A. 98844

Order a Bright Business Idea Book by Mail:

I would like to order the Bright Business Ideas book(s):

Bright Business Ideas   ❏

Bright Business Ideas II   ❏

_____ x $14.99 ea. + $2.00 per book = _____

| Quantity | Amount | Postage & Handling | Total Amount Enclosed |

(please print)

Name:_____

Street:_____

City: _____

Prov./State:_____Postal/Zip:_____

* Please make check/cheque or money order payable to:
  Bright Publishing Inc.
* Canadian residents add G.S.T.
* Orders outside Canada to be paid in U.S. funds by check/cheque
  or money order.
* Prices subject to change without prior notice.
* No C.O.D.'s please.

Gift Card Message

We will gladly enclose your personal message with the book sent as a gift. Write your message in the area provided below. Please put name of receiver on the order card above.

A GIFT FOR YOU

**Bright
Business
Ideas**

Bright Business Ideas
Compact Disc
"Information and Inspiration"

CASSETTE EXCHANGE OPTION:

To exchange the "Information and Inspiration" CD for a cassette, simply detach and mail the book page with the CD intact, (marked **Fragile**) to:

Bright Publishing Inc.	Bright Publishing Inc.
Box 24002, Lakefront P.O.	Room 261, Box 5000
Kelowna, British Columbia	Oroville, Washington
Canada V1Y 9P9	U.S.A. 98844

I would like to exchange my "Information and Inspiration" CD for a cassette of the same title.

<u>Enclosed</u>	x	<u>$00.00</u>	+	<u>$2.00 per item</u>	=	_____
CD		Cassette Amount		Handling & Postage		Total Amount Enclosed

I would like to order, without an exchange, the "Information and Inspiration":

CD ☐
Cassette ☐

_____	x	<u>$10.99</u>	+	<u>$2.00 per item</u>	=	_____
Quantity		Amount		Handling & Postage		Total Amount Enclosed

(please print)

Name:_____

Street:_____

City: _____

Prov./State:_____Postal/Zip:_____

- Please make check/cheque or money order payable to: Bright Publishing Inc.
- Canadian residents add G.S.T.
- Orders outside Canada to be paid in U.S. funds by check/cheque or money order.
- Prices subject to change without prior notice.
- No C.O.D.'s please.

The Perfect Gift for Father's Day, Birthdays, Graduation or Any Occasion